NATIVE AMERICAN LIFE

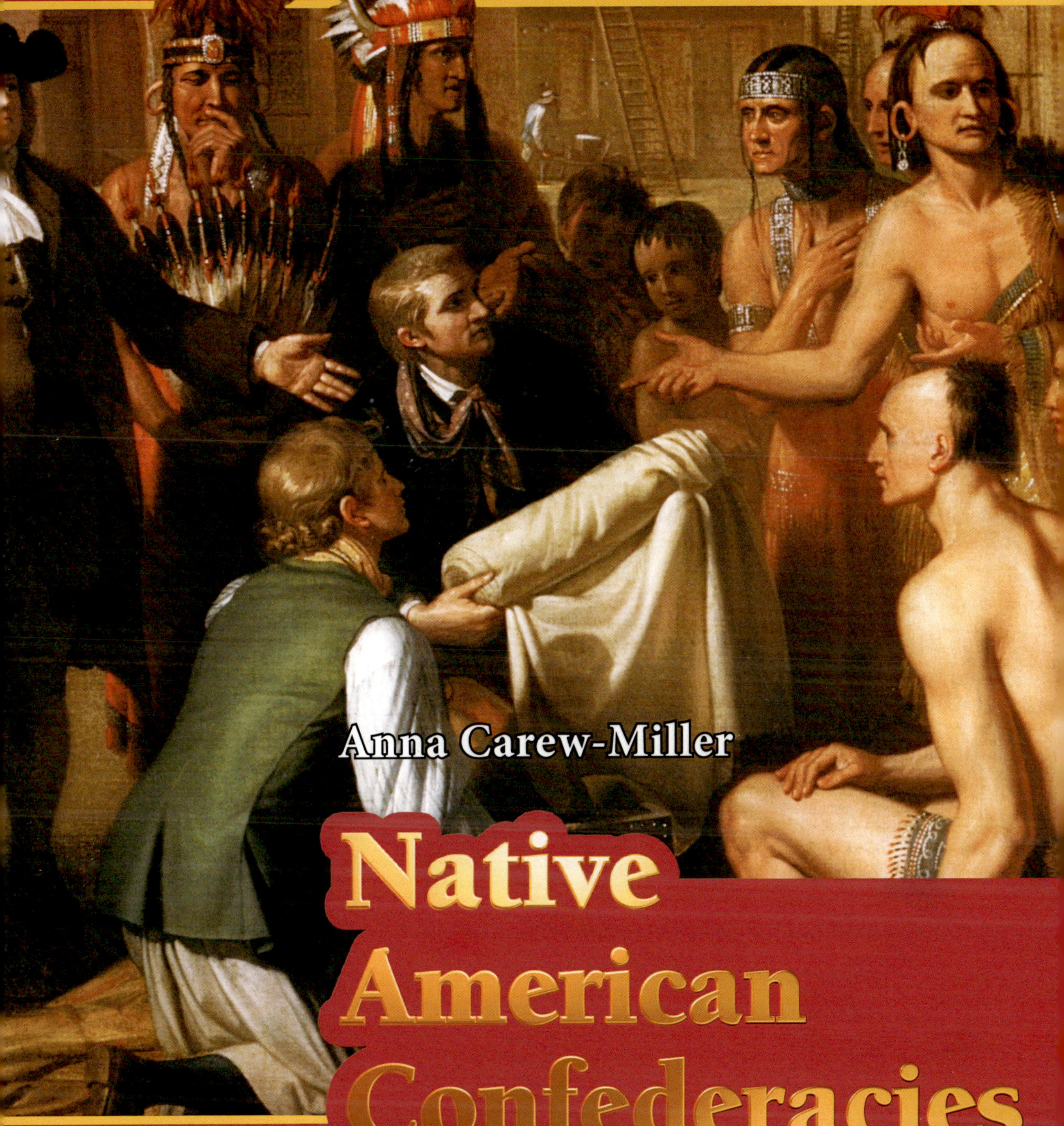

Anna Carew-Miller

Native American Confederacies

LIGHTBOX
openlightbox.com

LIGHTBOX

Go to **www.openlightbox.com** and enter this book's unique code.

ACCESS CODE

LBXW2497

Lightbox is an all-inclusive digital solution for the teaching and learning of curriculum topics in an original, groundbreaking way. Lightbox is based on National Curriculum Standards.

STANDARD FEATURES OF LIGHTBOX

AUDIO High-quality narration using text-to-speech system

ACTIVITIES Printable PDFs that can be emailed and graded

SLIDESHOWS Pictorial overviews of key concepts

VIDEOS Embedded high-definition video clips

WEBLINKS Curated links to external, child-safe resources

TRANSPARENCIES Step-by-step layering of maps, diagrams, charts, and timelines

INTERACTIVE MAPS Interactive maps and aerial satellite imagery

QUIZZES Ten multiple choice questions that are automatically graded and emailed for teacher assessment

KEY WORDS Matching key concepts to their definitions

CONTENTS

The Chacoan People built massive public buildings that demonstrated their engineering skills. The ruins of these buildings can be seen at the Chaco Culture National Historical Park.

Native American Confederacies

Today, Native American Nations are seen as both political groupings and cultural groupings. In the past, however, a Nation was a group of **indigenous** people who were connected by common rituals, beliefs, and language. A **confederacy** was an **alliance** between two or more Native American Nations.

Although many confederacies were created as a result of European contact, with member Nations uniting against a common enemy, there were confederacies prior to European contact. Archeological evidence suggests that a confederacy may have been what created the Chacoan culture, which existed in northern New Mexico from about 950 AD to 1100 AD. These people flourished in the desert for a couple of hundred years, building adobe structures, but then disappeared.

The Mound Builders, who lived in walled towns near the Mississippi River, were another complex society that seems to have involved a confederacy. The culture flourished from about 900 AD to 1600 AD, but started to break down before the Spanish arrived. After the Spanish conquest of the Southeast, Mississippian culture completely collapsed. However, anthropologists believe that the beliefs and social customs survived in the Nations that emerged afterward, such as the Creeks.

After the Europeans came, the social and political organization of Native Americans changed. Europeans brought diseases with them. The native peoples had little resistance to these diseases, and many of them died. Such loss caused tribes, clans, and bands of native people to reorganize. The arrival of the Europeans also created hostilities that led to bloodshed. These further losses caused the Nations to reorganize again.

In the past, some Nations had worked together to maintain their territory and fight off other, more powerful, Nations. However, with the coming of the Europeans, they faced a new kind of power and a new way of thinking about land and its possession. Native Americans did not believe they could own the land, whereas the Europeans thought of land as a possession.

In many regions, Native American groups banded together in confederacies to deal with this new enemy. They had to negotiate and decide who they were in relation to other groups and the territory they occupied. The formation of confederacies allowed Native Peoples, for a time, to face the power of the Europeans.

Strength in Unity

In the 1600s, the leaders of the Chumash People on the California coast created a political system enabling them to deal with the Spanish as a unified people. Previously, the Chumash had lived as independent bands, based on clans and extended families. Once the Spanish arrived, the Chumash created a council uniting all the separate groups. The council was an assembly of 20 leaders, and was led by one leader. This system worked while Chumash lived in separate communities. However, when the Chumash moved into the Spanish missions, diseases wiped them out.

Accounts relating to the sale of Manhattan Island to Dutch settlers vary. One version is that, in May 1626, a group of Native Americans traded the island for 60 guilders, or about US$972.

A group of smaller Nations formed the Wappinger Confederacy in response to the Dutch coming into their territory, which spread along the east bank of the Hudson River, to the tip of what is now Manhattan, to Poughkeepsie and into western Connecticut. Early in the 17th century, this confederacy had nearly 5,000 members. The power of the Wappinger Confederacy broke, however, after a war with the Dutch in the 1640s.

The 18th century was a time of **treaties** between Native American confederacies and Europeans. The big treaty issue was trade. The American Revolution was a disaster for the powerful confederacies, such as the Iroquois and the Creeks, as it became impossible for these confederacies to fight the unified power of the United States.

In the 19th century, many of the old confederacies fell apart. As Peoples from the east coast of the United States were pushed west, competition for land, as well as disease and violence, led to political reorganization among tribal groups. New confederacies rose and fell. Only in the 20th century would new confederacies give Native American Peoples power and a voice in the political landscape of the United States.

7,000 square miles (18,130 square km)
The size of **Chumash Territory** in California. It stretched from Malibu to Paso Robles, and across to the San Joaquin valley.

15,000
The number of years since the **first humans** arrived in America, by crossing a land bridge from **Asia**

17,000
The number of **Native Americans** in North Dakota killed in 1837 by smallpox, a disease that was brought by the Europeans and almost wiped out several Nations

The Iroquois developed their system of government at a series of councils attended by their leaders, including Hayenwatha. It is thought that their ideals influenced Benjamin Franklin and the writers of the U.S. Constitution.

The Northeast: The Iroquois League

One of the oldest and most powerful confederacies was the Iroquois League. This confederacy was based on internal peace and the shared belief of respect for ancestors, warriors, and clan mothers. Its people spoke five different **dialects**, and belonged to five different tribes: Onondaga, Cayuga, Oneida, Mohawk, and Seneca. They lived in more than 200 villages in what is now upper New York and southern Ontario. They called themselves the People of the Long House, or Hodenosaunee, because of the style of structure in which their **matriarchal**, extended families lived.

According to oral histories, the Iroquois League was formed around 1450. These stories explain that, before the league was formed, there was constant war among the Nations of this region. The battles began to have an impact on the population and culture. This worried some wise men in these Nations.

The founders of the confederacy were Hayenwatha, an Onondaga leader struggling to reform his Nation, and Deganawidah, a Huron prophet known as the Peacemaker. Deganawidah believed that these warring Peoples must unite under the roots of the Great Tree of Peace, a tall pine tree. The pine tree, with its spreading roots, represented a unified society. Deganawidah believed that the people must live in harmony and justice by forming a government. Together, the two men traveled from village to village with their message of brotherhood and equality. Eventually, all five Nations agreed to accept this idea.

The Iroquois League was an early form of **democratic** government, which balanced local interests with those of the league as a whole. Its territory covered the area from the Hudson River to Lake Erie. This land was divided into north-south strips, each governed by its own tribal council. The senior women chose men to represent their clans at village councils. Each Nation lived in independent villages. The Iroquois League council did not interfere with the affairs of individual Nations.

It was decided that the Onondagas would be the "fire keepers." This meant that they maintained the symbolic fire around which the council met. The league's great councils were held in an Onondaga village because these were the most centrally located. The senior women chose 49 council chiefs who met with the league as a whole. These representatives made all council decisions unanimously. The council usually met every summer, although its law said it had to meet only once every five years.

For almost 200 years, the Iroquois League existed for peace, not war. Only on rare occasions did it unite all five Nations to fight an external enemy. However, the coming of the Europeans changed all that. The league tried to remain neutral as the British and French grew increasingly hostile toward each other. However, the league's neutrality was not perfect. Groups of warriors, or even whole Nations, would sometimes fight the British or the French.

Iroquois Village
The Iroquois lived in permanent villages. A number of related families lived in each longhouse. Inside, the walls were lined with benches. Each family had its own section of the longhouse, and shared a fire pit with one other family.

By the end of the 18th century, the Iroquois League had about 16,000 members, which made it a powerful force for the Europeans to deal with. However, as with other Nations, its members suffered because of European diseases. To combat this, and increase population numbers, it replaced dead family members by adopting captive members of enemy Peoples. In addition, the league's numbers grew as remnants of Nations destroyed by disease or conquest were adopted into the five tribes of the league. In 1722, the Tuscarora Nation joined the Iroquois League after being pushed out of North Carolina by British colonials, becoming the sixth member.

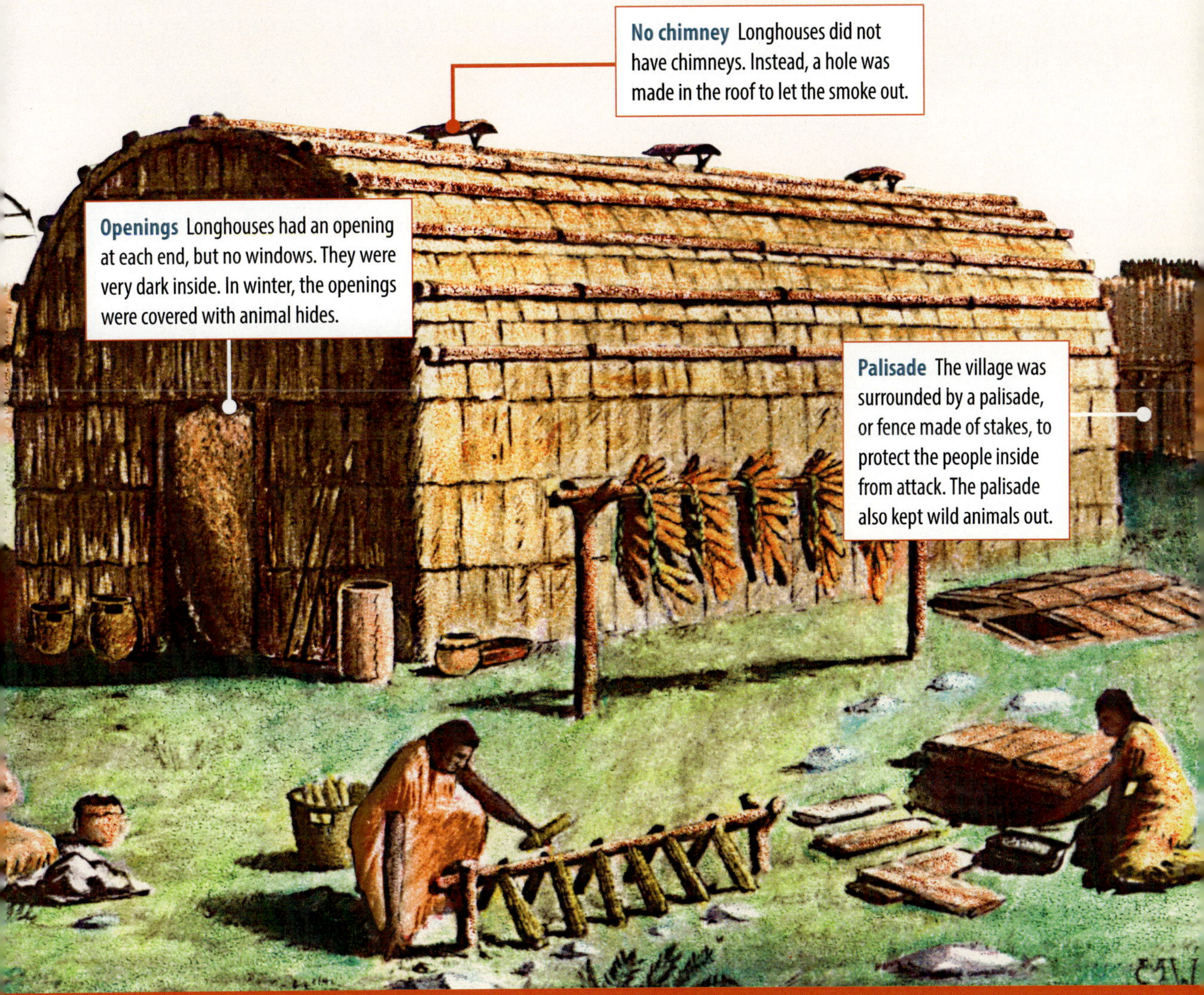

Because of its numbers and its tradition of members working together, the Iroquois League became the critical Native American group in the **imperial** wars of the 18th century. During the 17th and 18th centuries, it presented a powerful united front in the face of European conquest. The British and the French both believed that the confederacy held the balance of power, and both tried to make alliances with it.

During this time, the Iroquois closed their lands in New York to armies and war parties of the French and their Native American allies, so the French could not attack New England. This tactic earned them the support of the British. However, the French kept trying to win over the Iroquois, creating a strong pro-French **faction** within the league. Staying neutral and finding agreement within council meetings became more and more difficult.

Wampum Belt

Hayenwatha is said to have started the custom of the wampum belt as a negotiating tool. A wampum belt was a string of shells, which represented a chain of connection between the five Iroquois League Nations.

In the mid-18th century, the Iroquois broke their neutrality and made a treaty with the British, giving away lands that were the territory of the Delaware, one of the Nations that depended on the league's protection. The Delaware had been part of the Covenant Chain, a league of peace and friendship between the Iroquois and other groups, including the British. This betrayal caused many other Nations to distrust the power of the league. The French soon found many allies among Nations that were happy to see the Iroquois challenged.

The supremacy of the Iroquois League in the Northeast ended with the American Revolution. This war weakened the league because the governing council had refused to take sides. The individual Nations joined the British, except for the Oneida, which joined the colonials. At the war's end, the victorious American government treated the Iroquois League as a defeated enemy. As a result, the league lost control of much of its territory and, more important, it lost its power as a confederacy.

Today, most Iroquois have adopted a western way of life. However, many also work to preserve their culture by maintaining their oral tradition and taking part in traditional ceremonies.

However, the Iroquois League did not disappear. Its remnants survived on small reservations into the 19th century. Today, the league is called the Iroquois Nation, and it is one of the strongest tribal organizations in the Northeast, dedicated to preserving its members' cultural heritage and protecting the civil rights of Native Peoples.

125,000
The number of **Iroquois today**

117
The number of **articles** in the Iroquois **Confederacy constitution**

50 to 150 feet (15 to 46 meters)
The length of **Iroquois longhouses**, which could be home to as many as 60 people

Pleasant Porter was the last elected principal chief of the Creek Nation. He was chair of the Creek commission that negotiated with the federal government about the allocation of land.

The Southeast: The Creek Confederacy

The Creeks were the descendants of the Mound Builder and Mississippian cultures. They got their English name "Creeks" because they often lived in the deep woods along creek beds. The Creek Confederacy that emerged in the 17th century included remnants of the Muskogee, Yuchi, Coweta, Alabama, Coosa, and Tuskegee Nations, as well as some Shawnee bands. Some of these Peoples did not even speak the same language, but they shared many cultural traditions and were united by the land they considered home.

The Creek Confederacy had no permanent central government, but evolved into a democratic and **communal** society. Like their Mound Builder ancestors, the Creeks lived in towns, called talwas. Each talwa was independent, but they all made decisions together. In the 18th century, there were about 50 of these towns. Each talwa would select a micco, or headman, to be part of the central council and deal with outsiders.

In the 18th century, the Creeks were caught between the British to the east, the Spanish to the south, and the French to the west. They negotiated with the European powers for trade, and maintained their homelands. Their talwas were like small nation-states existing alongside the settlements of the young American republic, and making treaties with the new federal government.

In the 18th century, there were many different factions within the Creek Confederacy. Some talwas allied with the British, others with the French or Spanish. However, the central council of miccos would meet and make important decisions together, uniting the confederacy. While the European governments wanted to divide the Creek Confederacy to make it less powerful, the miccos of the Creeks often played off one European power against another.

After the American Revolution, the Creek Confederacy became more unified because of increased white settlement. The United States government made treaties with the Creeks, but the states where the Creeks' lands existed did not always recognize the federal treaties. Thus, the Creek Confederacy had trouble with Georgia and Alabama, the states that contained their traditional homelands. The state governments ignored the federal treaties and seized Creek lands for settlers.

Creek Statesman

Alexander McGillivray was an important figure in the history of the Creek Confederacy. A Creek statesman, who died in 1793, he was the son of a Scottish father and a Creek mother from Ochiapofa, in what is now Georgia. McGillivray became a great diplomat at the end of the 18th century. He persuaded the towns of the Creek Confederacy to develop a unified foreign policy, and he made the central council more active. In 1770, McGillivray helped to formulate the Treaty of New York. In this treaty, the United States government pledged to protect the Creek Confederacy from outside settlement within its boundaries. When he was asked to approve a bad treaty with the state of Georgia, McGillivray said: "Our lands are our life and breath. If we part with them, we part with our blood."

The forced removal of Native American Peoples from their lands in the Southeast to present-day Oklahoma became known as the Trail of Tears.

After the War of 1812, the Creeks began to lose power as a confederacy. The United States government was not interested in negotiating for trade purposes. Land was the issue. Even though the Creeks had adapted to live like their settler neighbors, they were seen as separate from the new country that was taking shape in their homelands. They were often treated badly by settlers, but they had no legal status that would allow them to protest these abuses.

By 1820, Georgia and Alabama, the states where the Creeks lived, put great pressure on the Creek Confederacy to move west of the Mississippi River. Living within these states was difficult for the Creeks, as Native Americans were not considered citizens of states. Many other Peoples faced the same problem. As a way of maintaining tribal **sovereignty** and security, the federal government offered removal to tribal lands in "Indian Territory," in what is now Oklahoma.

Throughout the 1820s, the miccos of the Creek Confederacy realized that resisting the United States was too destructive. Many of them agreed to sign the Indian Removal Treaty in 1834. However, not all the Creek communities agreed to leave for Indian Territory. By the 19th century, those Creeks and the remnants of other tribes who had avoided removal had become the Seminole Nation in Florida. They lived deep in the inland swamps in regions that white settlers did not care about.

After the removal to Oklahoma, the Creek Confederacy banded together as a single tribe, calling themselves the Muskogee Nation. They were among the 42 Nations that the United States government relocated to Indian Territory during this period. The Muskogee Nation was part of what was known as the Five Civilized Tribes in Indian Territory. The others were the Cherokees, Chickasaws, Choctaws, and Seminoles. These Nations were called the Five Civilized Tribes because they had adapted to European culture before their removal. They often converted to Christianity, lived in European-style houses, and raised livestock. Some even owned slaves.

The Seminoles of Florida had distinctive clothing. The men usually wore a colorful, cotton shirt and a turban headdress.

During the Civil War, the Muskogee Nation was divided, much as the entire U.S. population was. However, after the Civil War, the Creek Peoples united once again. In 1867, the tribal leaders wrote a new constitution for the Muskogee Nation, modeled on the Constitution of the United States.

In 1887, the Dawes Severalty Act broke up the various reservations that had allowed each Nation to hold its land in common. This law forced each tribal member to take an **allotment**, a small portion of what had originally been tribally owned land. Thus, the Muskogee Nation no longer had a homeland. This had a terrible effect on its power and identity, as it no longer had the ability to control the destiny of its people.

In spite of this blow to the culture of the Creek Confederacy, the Creeks managed to survive because of their hardiness and adaptability. Today, the Muskogee Nation exists as a political body. It safeguards the rights and customs of what was once a diverse group of people.

System for Writing

One member of the Five Civilized Tribes, Sequoyah (1760–1843), created a Cherokee syllabary, which is a set of characters representing a syllable. This enabled Cherokees to read and write in their own language.

One-Third
The portion of the Cherokee population that **died** on the **Trail of Tears**

1828
The year that the *Cherokee Phoenix*, the **first Native American newspaper**, began publication

4,000–6,000
The number of people today who **can speak Muskogee**, which is the main language of the Creek Confederacy

The Spanish gave the name *Pueblo* to the town-dwelling Peoples of the Southwest. Pueblo means "town" or "people" in Spanish.

The Southwest: The Pueblos

All of the Pueblo Peoples had a strongly related culture, but four different languages were spoken among them. Some of the Pueblos may have been the descendants of the ancient Peoples who had inhabited the ruins of Chaco Canyon. Each Pueblo People lived in a village, or group of villages, surrounded by their farmland and hunting territory. The Western Pueblos, found in western New Mexico and eastern Arizona, were the Hopi, Zuñi, Acoma, and Laguna. The Eastern Pueblos lived near or along the Rio Grande. They were the Taos, Isleta, Jemez, San Juan, San Ildefonso, Cochiti, Zia, Santa Ana, Santa Clara, San Felipe, and Santo Domingo.

In many ways, the relationship among the Pueblos did not fit the definition of a confederacy. Although they rarely had conflicts with each other, they did not usually cooperate with each other, either. Each community was independent, and organized by spiritual leaders who controlled various aspects of the community. This diversity and independence from each other was a weakness when the Spanish came.

Francisco Vásquez de Coronado, searching for legendary cities of gold, raided Pueblo towns along the Rio Grande in 1540. Many of the Pueblos resisted individually when the Spanish soldiers seized their food supplies. However, there was no confederacy or alliance that bound the Pueblos together against a common enemy.

In 1598, the Spanish king gave Juan de Oñate a land grant to New Mexico. De Oñate came north from Mexico with colonists, missionary Catholic priests, and soldiers, to begin his attempt at establishing a permanent colony. At first, the Pueblos tolerated these intruders. The holy men at San Juan Pueblo gave the colonists a place to live in one of their towns, which the Spanish renamed San Gabriel.

However, the Pueblos soon had many reasons to wish for an end to the Spanish colony. The primary cause was religion. The Spanish missionaries who had accompanied the colonists forced the Pueblos to convert to Catholicism. The Spanish priests did not understand the spiritual practices of the Pueblos, and believed these people were doomed if they were not baptized. Those who openly resisted conversion to this European religion were treated harshly, and sometimes even killed.

The Pueblos' other major complaint was that they were forced to supply the colonists with food and labor. This was a practice that the Spanish had begun in their colonies in Mexico and South America. The system that required the Pueblos to give part of their crops to Spanish settlement leaders was known as *encomienda*. The system that required the Pueblos to work in Spanish fields was known as *repartimiento*.

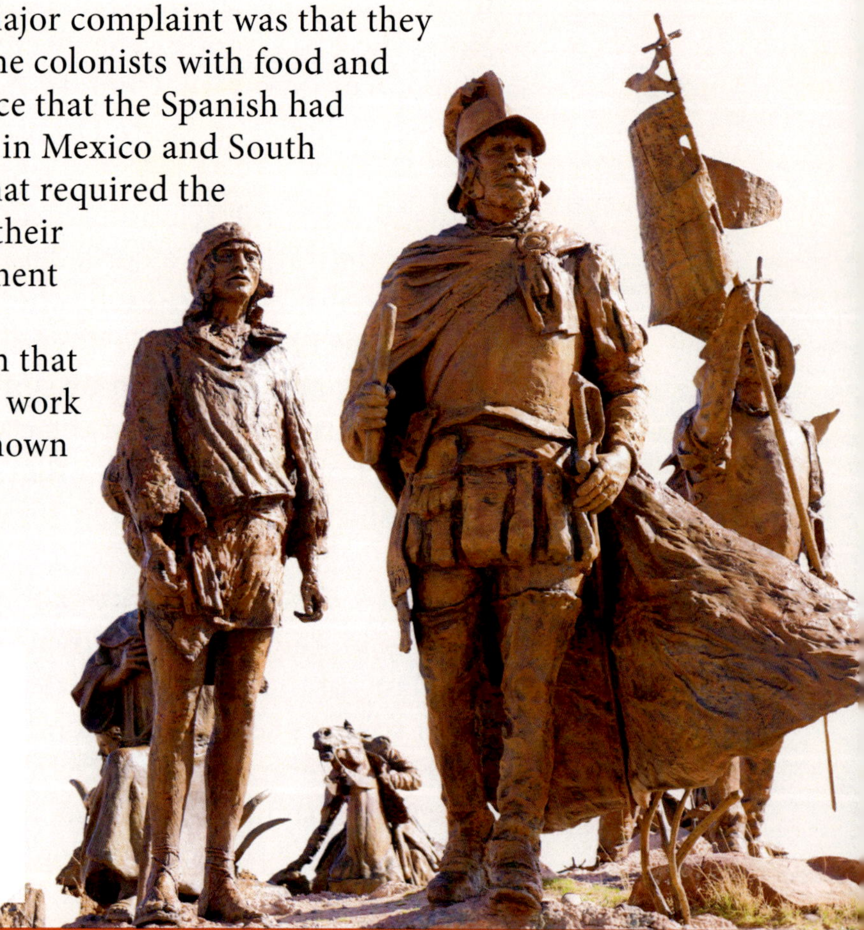

Juan de Oñate and 400 settlers crossed the Rio Grande at El Paso, to establish the Spanish colony of New Mexico. In 1613, Oñate was charged with cruelty and false reporting as governor, and banished from New Mexico.

In spite of the forced assistance from the Pueblos, the Spanish colony failed. Most of the group returned to Mexico in 1606. In 1610, the rest relocated to Santa Fe. With more land grants settled, the Spanish made greater demands on the Pueblos for food and labor. Bitterness and resentment against the Spanish colony grew.

The alliance that developed among the Pueblos was the direct result of their mistreatment by the Spanish. By the late 17th century, the holy men had begun to organize the confederacy. Their goal was to eliminate the Spanish from their homeland.

A leader from San Juan Pueblo, named Popé, became the major figure in the rebellion against the Spanish. In 1674, Popé was one of 47 leaders arrested by the Spanish for **sorcery**. They were taken to Santa Fe for trial. Four were hanged. Popé and the rest were whipped.

Historical records show that Popé was a powerful person. He defied the Spanish by practicing his own religion, and had been the war captain of his village.

This experience may have motivated Popé to unite the Pueblos against the Spanish. To devise a plan, Popé called meetings in anti-Spanish villages. However, Popé's resistance movement had enemies among the Pueblos, and he had to leave his village of San Juan for his own safety. He went to Taos, and, with allies from every Pueblo, developed the plan for the Pueblo Revolt of 1680.

Popé's plan almost failed. Pro-Spanish Pueblos informed the Spanish priests who ran the missions. This caused some of the messengers—who ran with secret letters between the Pueblos—to be arrested by the Spanish. Popé immediately put the plan of attack into action.

The Spanish were able to retreat into Santa Fe, but the Pueblo warriors laid siege to the settlement. During the attack, half of the 800 Spanish colonists were killed, and most of their livestock slaughtered. The siege ended when the Pueblo warriors drove the remaining Spanish down the Rio Grande to El Paso.

The Socorro Mission in Texas was established to provide refuge for Pueblo and Spanish people fleeing from the Pueblo Revolt.

The Pueblo Revolt was the only time Spain lost part of its empire to Native Americans whom it had previously conquered. Diego de Vargas, who retook the territory, inscribed his feat on El Morro Rock in New Mexico.

The triumph of the revolt and the fear of a counterattack by the Spanish kept the confederacy together for several years afterward. During this time, Pueblo holy men urged the Pueblos to give up European goods and habits. Under Popé's leadership, they held rituals to "unbaptize" the converts to Christianity, and urged a return to the old ways.

Popé let his success go to his head and had those who opposed him killed. He didn't enjoy his power for long. After his death, the Pueblo alliance collapsed. In 1692, the Spanish returned in force and were able to reoccupy the region. Only the most western Pueblos of the Hopi were not part of the reconquest. This time, the Spanish learned from their past mistakes and did not try to impose their culture with violence. The Spanish and the Pueblo Peoples learned how to live alongside each other.

An annual fiesta in Santa Fe commemorates the return of the Spanish to the town in 1692.

Under Spanish rule, the Pueblos had to give up some of their independence. They became subjects of the Spanish king, and they were baptized at birth and attended Catholic Mass. However, they also maintained their traditional spiritual ceremonies.

For their part, the Spanish did not interfere with Pueblo leadership, and Pueblo towns continued to be governed by traditional clan leaders and holy men. Eventually, the Spanish began to rely on the Pueblos as allies against the **nomadic** Native American Nations, such as the Apache, Navajo, and Comanche.

The long-term consequence of reconquest by the Spanish was that the Pueblos made political decisions independently. Their rural villages functioned like states. When the United States took control of the territory from Mexico in the 1840s, the Pueblos were allowed to remain in their homelands. As a result, they avoided the economic problems that other reservations had in the 19th century.

In 1921, the confederacy united once again, to oppose the Bursum Bill, which threatened to give Pueblo lands to non-Native Americans and proposed to limit Pueblo religious practices. Elected members from every Pueblo formed the All Pueblo Council. "We must unite as we did once before," said one of the leaders. This was the first time the Pueblos had united for political purposes since 1680. Their efforts led to the defeat of the bill in 1922.

Although fiercely independent, the Pueblo Peoples have continued to support each other. They band together for political influence and economic purposes while maintaining the individuality of each Pueblo community.

Having lived in the Southwest for thousands of years, the Pueblo Peoples have a strong attachment to their homeland.

Native American Heritage Centers

Throughout the United States, cultural centers and museums have been established to inform people about Native American Nations, and to celebrate Native American cultures. Some of them feature Nations mentioned in this book.

Ah-Tah-Thi-Ki Museum, Clewiston, Florida

The museum has more than 180,000 artifacts relating to the Seminole.

Lompoc Museum, Lompoc, California

Exhibits showing Chumash life are part of this museum.

Indian Pueblo Cultural Center, Albuquerque, New Mexico

The art and culture of New Mexico's 19 pueblos are shown at this center.

New Amsterdam History Center, Manhattan Island, New York

Native American relations with early settlers are explored at this center.

Iroquois Indian Museum, Howes Cave, New York

This museum focuses on using art to showcase Iroquois culture.

Ocmulgee National Monument, Maco, Georgia

This monument highlights prehistoric Native American life.

The arrival of horses on the Great Plains changed the life of the Native Americans there. Hunting buffalo became much easier, meaning that, among other things, the food supply became more reliable.

The Great Plains and High Plateau: The Blackfoot Confederacy

The Blackfoot Confederacy included the Blackfoot (Siksika), Blood (Kainah), Piegan (Pikuni), and Small Robe Peoples. Blackfoot is a British term, used because these people used to dye their moccasins black. In their own language, the Blackfoot call themselves Amskapi Pikuni. Although their wanderings often separated the confederacy, these Nations shared customs and language. They often intermarried. The confederacy came together for traditional ceremonies or to defend each other against common enemies.

Some archeological evidence suggests that these Nations lived in their homeland in the upper Missouri River region for thousands of years. Other scholars believe they were originally village dwellers in Minnesota who moved onto the Plains. They may have been displaced by eastern Nations moving west or by settlers, or they may have moved in pursuit of the furs that were part of their livelihood. However, by the mid-18th century, they had horses, and had become nomadic people of the Plains, following the buffalo.

Decorative headgear was part of the ceremonial clothing used in the Sun Dance.

The languages of the Blackfoot Confederacy were part of the Algonquian language group, spoken by many Peoples of the Northeast, suggesting that they were once part of the same group of people. The Nations of the confederacy were ruled by chiefs. Followers paid tribute, in the form of food and other objects, to their powerful leaders, who redistributed it to the needy or used it in ceremonies of thanksgiving. Their only cultivated crop was tobacco, which they used for ceremonies.

The important rituals for the Nations of the Blackfoot Confederacy were the Sun Dance and the vision quest. Among the Native American Peoples of the eastern woodlands and the Great Plains areas, the vision quest was an important part of a boy's initiation into adulthood. The boy went out from the encampment by himself, spending days in prayer and **fasting** so he could discover some sign of his guardian spirit.

The Sun Dance was the most important religious ceremony for many Great Plains Peoples. It was held once a year, in early summer. With the Sun Dance, members of the Blackfoot Confederacy would gather and confirm their basic beliefs about the universe and the spirit world.

For the Blackfoot, lakes and rivers had special powers. They were home to the beaver. This animal was almost as important as the buffalo. In the 1700s, the Peoples of the Blackfoot Confederacy came to depend on fur trading, especially the trade in beaver pelts. Fur trading appears to have changed the culture of the Blackfoot Peoples. Successful hunters began to take on more than one wife. They had many horses, and they needed several wives to prepare the abundance of furs for trade.

The Blackfoot Confederacy was known for its hostility toward neighboring Nations and Europeans. When Lewis and Clark traveled through Native American territory in 1806, the Blackfoot were the only Native Americans to attack the party. Blackfoot Peoples fought often with the neighboring Shoshone, Flathead, Kutenai, and Snake Peoples. Being a successful warrior was an important part of their culture.

The Blackfoot Confederacy was one of several alliances among the Peoples of the Plains and High Plateau regions. The Pawnee Confederacy rose to power in the late 18th century, carrying out raids against enemies to the east and west. In the 19th century, a loose alliance among the Sioux, Arapaho, and Cheyenne dominated the northern Plains. These Nations were challenged by the Blackfoot and Pawnee Confederations.

Native Americans used the whole buffalo. They preserved the meat so it would last through winter. They used the skin for shelter, clothing, and shoes, and the stomach as a container. They made soap from the fat, and utensils from the bone.

Plains warriors had a system by which their acts of bravery were recorded. The greatest honor went to a warrior who got close enough to touch an enemy, dead or alive, and escape without injury.

On the eastern edge of the Plains, the Mandan, Arikara, and Hidatsa Peoples were known as the three **affiliated** Nations. These village-dwelling Peoples worked in mutual defense against raids from their nomadic neighbors to the west and in conflicts with white settlers to the east.

During the 18th century, the Blackfoot Confederacy thrived. Its members traded furs for guns with British trading companies in Canada, such as the Hudson Bay Company, and, with their horses, hunted buffalo on the vast northern Plains. However, as settlers from the United States began to push through their territory in the upper Missouri River region in the 19th century, the fiercely independent Blackfoot Confederacy began to change.

First, disease took its toll. In 1837, a smallpox epidemic killed nearly two-thirds of the Blackfoot, more than 6,000 people. The disease spread as people, who were infected at a white trading post, returned to their bands. Only a few members of the Small Robe Nation survived, but the Nation disappeared forever as the survivors were absorbed into the other Nations of the Blackfoot Confederacy.

Then, the buffalo began to disappear. Buffalo were the major source of food, clothing, and shelter for the Blackfoot Confederacy, but white hunters cut down the herds far more quickly than Native American hunters. By 1883, the buffalo had been nearly exterminated. As a result, many members of the confederacy starved to death that winter.

Eventually, the confederacy's homelands in Canada and the United States caught the eye of white settlers. While the Blackfoot Confederacy avoided a major military confrontation with the United States Army, until the end of the 19th century it resisted signing treaties forcing its members to give up their homelands. In 1896, Blackfoot leaders finally signed an agreement with the United States government, giving up territory that eventually became Glacier National Park in Montana.

The Blackfoot had a reputation as warlike, and at first viewed fur traders as poachers. Later, however, they not only traded furs themselves but also supplied food to the traders.

Archeologists have recently discovered that people have lived in the region of Glacier National Park for about 10,000 years. These were probably ancestors of the Blackfoot and other Plains Nations.

During the late 1800s, the Blackfoot Confederacy lost its power as a political force. It also lost much of its culture, as reservation life and the boarding schools that the government required the children to attend challenged Blackfoot traditions. However, in the past 50 years, the Blackfoot have seen a revival in their culture. Today, more than 8,000 members of the Blackfoot Nation live on their reservation in Montana, sustaining their traditions while looking toward the future.

100s
The number of **buffalo** left at the beginning of the **20th century**, as a result of white settlers slaughtering them

20 Fishhooks
The value of **one male beaver skin**, which could also be exchanged for
1 pair of shoes, or
1 blanket, or 2 shirts,
or 2 hatchets, or
8 knives, or
144 buttons

30 Million
The number of **buffalo** when Europeans arrived in America

Warrior and Peacemaker

An important figure in the history of the Blackfoot Confederacy is Crowfoot, a leader and peacemaker who was born around 1821 into the Blood Nation. In his youth, Crowfoot saw smallpox epidemics devastate his people. His father, Chief Many Names, most likely died of smallpox in the 1837 epidemic.

Crowfoot was not raised for peace. A saying in his warrior culture was: "Better to die young as a brave warrior than to get old." By the time he was a young man, Crowfoot had fought in 19 battles, mostly with other Nations. By his 30s, he had become a tribal leader known for his skills as a speaker and for his levelheaded approach to solving conflicts.

Helping his people survive was Crowfoot's greatest challenge as a leader. When the buffalo began to disappear and the numbers of white settlers in his people's homeland increased, he realized that the Blackfoot Confederacy was outnumbered and survival depended upon working with the Europeans, not resisting them. In the 1870s, Crowfoot became a spokesman for the confederacy, negotiating treaties with the governments of Canada and the United States. In 1877, he signed a treaty with Canada that gave up much territory, a decision that may have saved lives but changed forever the way the confederacy lived.

Before Crowfoot died, he knew that life had gotten worse for his people, but, unlike some of their neighboring nations, they had survived. Crowfoot's last words reflect the sorrow and loss he suffered in his lifetime: "What is life? It is the flash of a firefly in the night. It is the breath of a buffalo in the winter time. It is the little shadow which runs across the grass and loses itself in the sunset."

In the 20th and 21st centuries, Native Americans have once again banded together in local, national, and pan-tribal organizations to protect their rights and preserve their cultures.

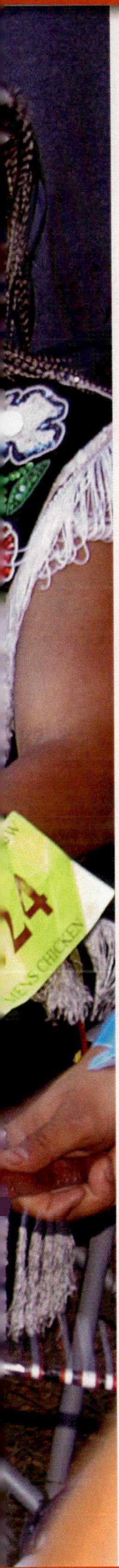

Modern Confederacies and Pan-Tribal Organizations

Native American confederacies were Nations that united for a common purpose. These tribes were usually neighbors. However, there have been times when a confederacy was **pan-tribal**. The sense of purpose that inspired some Nations' leaders to create large confederacies extending to all Native Peoples was their shared **enmity** toward the European invaders. In the 18th century, Pontiac, an Ottawa chieftain, tried to create an anti-British confederation that stretched from the Great Lakes to the Mississippi River. However, this confederation failed because of power struggles among the member Nations.

Two Shawnee leaders, Tecumseh and Tenskwatawa, began a movement in the early 19th century to unite the Peoples of the Ohio River valley. They envisioned an alliance that was both political and religious. Tecumseh took the side of the British in the War of 1812. However, the young American republic defeated these allies, and Tecumseh died at the Battle of the Thames.

Disruption has had a huge effect on the political organization of Native American life. In 1830, the Indian Removal Act forced most Eastern Peoples to move to Indian Territory. The strong confederacies of the East lost their power as they attempted to reorganize in their new homelands.

As European settlers continued to pour into the West, alliances among Western Peoples tried to hold back the tide. However, these Nations lost many battles and negotiations, and their lands were taken from them. They were then forced to live on reservations.

Reservations caused diverse tribes to come together as a single group. A good example can be found in the Confederated Tribes of the Warm Springs Reservation in central Oregon. The three main Nations that the government placed there were the Wasco, Paiute, and Sahaptin. Not only had these Peoples never lived together in the past, but they also spoke a number of different languages.

The Confederated Tribes of the Warm Springs Reservation don traditional dress for the annual Pi-Ume-Sha Days. The event commemorates the 1855 treaty in which their reservation was founded. Pi-Ume-Sha means "Let's celebrate" in the Sahaptin language.

The Confederated Tribes evolved into a fairly unified group, maintaining cultural traditions, such as sacred foods, seasonal feasts, and ceremonies. By 1938, the groups on the reservation had organized a tribal government, an 11-member council with an elected chief. The history of the Confederated Tribes demonstrates the ability of Native American Peoples to adapt while keeping their traditions alive.

By the end of the 19th century, the government was making even reservation lands available to settlers. Soon, the reservation system was under attack, and many reservations were broken and sold into private ownership. The alliances forged in hardship nearly disappeared.

Between 1880 and 1934, the U.S. government's policy toward Native Americans was one of **assimilation**. The goal was to integrate these people into larger society through education, by breaking up tribally held lands through allotment, and by granting individuals citizenship. **Tribalism** survived, however, and new confederacies emerged.

In the 20th century, many new Native American organizations formed. These groups strove for civil rights and **self-determination**. At times, they combined the interests of several Nations. The Alaska Native Brotherhood (1912) and the Alaska Native Sisterhood (1914) were dedicated to preserving Native culture and fighting discrimination of any kind. The California Indian Brotherhood (1926) organized various Nations to lobby for more land, better schools and health care, and compensation for lands taken in the 19th century.

The Alaska Native Brotherhood and Alaska Native Sisterhood hall in Sitka, Alaska, built in 1914, is a now national historic landmark. It is used for events such as Thanksgiving celebrations.

Some groups were pan-tribal. The Society of American Indians (1911) stressed that Native Americans should be involved in their own self-betterment. They wanted to clear up problems relating to the status of tribal sovereignty and American citizenship. Eventually, the group broke up because of disagreements, but it succeeded in changing the U.S. government's policy of assimilation. The Indian Reorganization Act of 1934 allowed tribes to have greater control over their identity.

The next group to attempt to address pan-tribal interests was the National Congress of American Indians (1944). Its members were the elected leaders of recognized Nations, and they were dedicated to lobbying on behalf of specific Peoples. Like other groups, they worked for voting rights and civil equality.

In the 1960s, the "Red Power" movement emerged. Its members were inspired by the activism of African Americans and Hispanic Americans. At first, its members were mostly young people who felt that, in spite of their traditional respect for the wisdom and leadership of their elders, these elders weren't acting in the best interests of Native Peoples.

The Confederation of American Indian Nations (1969) comprised mostly students. The group occupied Alcatraz, once a Native American homeland. It wanted to build a cultural center on the island.

The Confederation of American Indian Nations occupied Alcatraz for 19 months. The protestors were eventually removed by the government, but their action led to the government adopting a policy of self-determination for Native Americans.

The American Indian Movement (AIM) started in 1968 to help Native Americans in ghettos in places such as Minneapolis and Los Angeles. It helped young Native Americans to adjust to urban life without losing their cultural identity. AIM strongly opposed U.S. government policies toward Native Americans, sometimes resorting to violence, which made the group unpopular with some Native Americans. Today, AIM's major concerns are economic independence, religious freedom, treaty rights, cultural revitalization, and environmental protection.

In this century, a number of tribes have united informally to raise issues relating to the environment. In 2012, the Affiliated Tribes of Northwest Indians, representing 50 Nations in seven states, successfully opposed the building of a large coal terminal in Washington state. In 2017, people from many other Nations went to North Dakota to support the Standing Rock Sioux, who were protesting against an oil pipeline being built under a reservoir close to their reservation. A number of other movements led by Native Americans have also had a strong voice in environmental issues.

The Standing Rock Sioux and their supporters took their environmental protest all the way to Washington, D.C.

Timeline

1450
The Iroquois League is formed, comprising the Mohawk, Oneida, Onondaga, Cayuga, and Seneca Nations. The Tuscarora join in 1722.

1598
Juan de Oñate establishes a Spanish colony in New Mexico. He treats the Native Americans cruelly, and is later exiled from the colony.

1600s
The Creek Confederacy is formed. Its members speak different languages but share aspects of their cultures.

1680
The Pueblo Revolt takes place. This uprising by the usually peaceful Pueblos results in the overthrow of Spanish rule in New Mexico for 12 years.

1813
Tecumseh, the Shawnee leader of pan-tribal revolt, is killed in battle.

1830
Congress passes the Indian Removal Act.

1834
The Creek Confederacy signs the removal treaty. The suffering the people endure on their journey leads to it being called The Trail of Tears.

1887
Congress passes the Dawes Severalty Act, allowing for the break-up of reservations into individual allotments.

1934
Congress passes the Indian Reorganization Act, allowing Native American Nations greater self-determination.

1968
The American Indian Movement (AIM) is established, becoming a voice for the grievances of Native Americans. Its leadership officially disbands in 1978.

2013
According to the U.S. Census Bureau, more than 5.2 million people in the United States identify as Native American or Alaska Native.

Quiz

1 When did the Mound Builders culture flourish?

2 How many members did the Wappinger Confederacy have in the early 17th century?

3 What were the names of the six Nations in the Iroquois League?

4 What was a Creek town called?

5 How many people can speak Muskogee, the main language of the Creek Confederacy, today?

6 What does Spanish word "pueblo" mean in English?

7 Who was the leader of the 1680 Pueblo Revolt?

8 What was the most important ritual for the Great Plains Peoples?

9 What were the three affiliated Nations of the Great Plains?

10 What was the name of the organization whose members occupied Alcatraz in 1969?

Answers **1.** Between 900 and 1600 AD **2.** 5,000 **3.** Onondaga, Cayuga, Oneida, Mohawk, Seneca, and Tuscarora **4.** A talwa **5.** 4,000 to 6,000 **6.** "town" or "people" **7.** Popé **8.** The Sun Dance **9.** Mandan, Arikara, and Hidatsa **10.** Confederation of American Indian Nations

Key Words

affiliated: brought into close connection as a member or branch

alliance: a formal agreement between nations to cooperate for a specific purpose

allotment: a portion of land granted to Native Americans after the breakup of the reservations

assimilation: the merging of cultural traits from previously distinct cultural groups

communal: participated in, shared, or used in common by members of a group or community

confederacy: an alliance formed for a specific purpose

democratic: having political or social equality

dialects: varieties of language distinguished from other related varieties by special use of grammar or vocabulary, used by speakers who are separated by geography

enmity: active and typically mutual hatred

faction a party or group, usually within a government

fasting: going without food for a period of time

imperial: relating to an empire, such as Great Britain

indigenous: an original or native inhabitant

matriarchal: societies that are controlled by women

nomadic: a lifestyle in which people have no permanent home, but move in a traditional route in search of food for themselves or their livestock

pan-tribal: encompassing all tribes of the United States

self-determination: the freedom of a people to determine the way in which they will be governed

sorcery: the use of powers that come from evil spirits

sovereignty: the independent power or authority of a state

treaties: formal agreements between governments or states about peace, alliances, trade, or other relations

tribalism: strong loyalty to one's own group or tribe

Index

LIGHTBOX

SUPPLEMENTARY RESOURCES

Click on the plus icon found in the bottom left corner of each spread to open additional teacher resources.

- Download and print the book's quizzes and activities
- Access curriculum correlations
- Explore additional web applications that enhance the Lightbox experience

LIGHTBOX DIGITAL TITLES
Packed full of integrated media

VIDEOS

INTERACTIVE MAPS

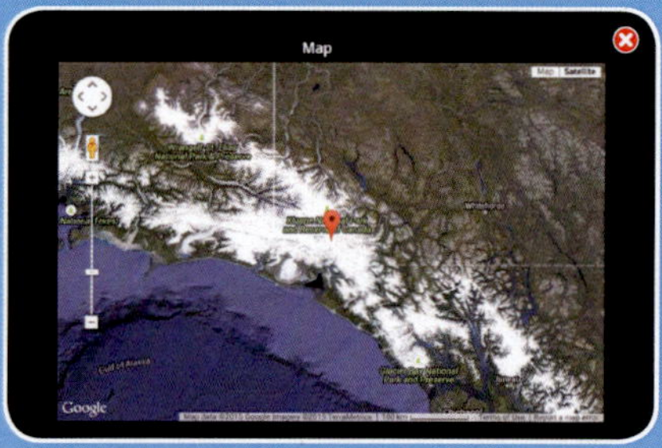

WEBLINKS

SLIDESHOWS

QUIZZES

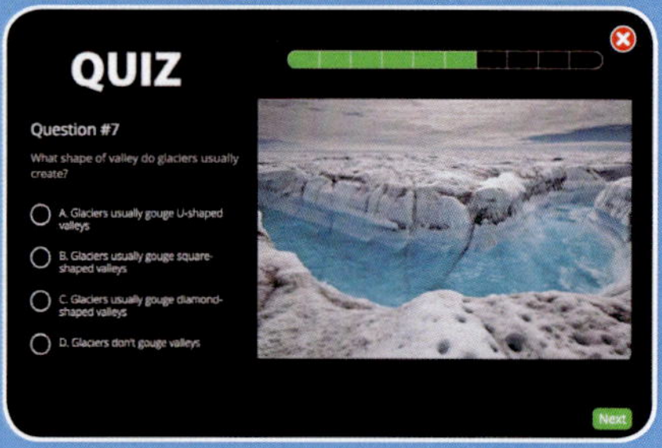

OPTIMIZED FOR
- ✔ TABLETS
- ✔ WHITEBOARDS
- ✔ COMPUTERS
- ✔ AND MUCH MORE!

Published by Smartbook Media Inc.
350 5th Avenue, 59th Floor New York, NY 10118
Website: www.openlightbox.com

First published by Mason Crest in 2014

Library of Congress Control Number: 2018941490

ISBN 978-1-5105-3936-5 (hardcover)
ISBN 978-1-5105-3935-8 (multi-user eBook)

Printed in the Brainerd, Minnesota, United States
1 2 3 4 5 6 7 8 9 0 22 21 20 19 18

062018
121117

Project Coordinator: Heather Kissock
Designer: Ana María Vidal

The publisher acknowledges Alamy, Getty Images, iStock, and Bridgeman Images as the primary image suppliers for this title.